MAR 2 8 2017

# Flying Lemur

### by Dee Phillips

**Consultants:**

**Greg Byrnes, PhD**
Assistant Professor of Biology, Siena College, New York

**Kimberly Brenneman, PhD**
National Institute for Early Education Research, Rutgers University, New Brunswick, New Jersey

BEARPORT
PUBLISHING

New York, New York

**Credits**
Cover, © Patrice Correia/Biosphoto/FLPA; 2–3, © David Yeo/Getty Images; 4, © Suzi Eszterhas/Minden Pictures/
FLPA; 5, © Tim Laman/National Geographic Stock; 7, © Patrice Correia/Biosphoto/FLPA; 8, © Tim Laman/ National
Geographic Stock; 9, © David Yeo/Getty Images; 10–11, © Andrea & Antonella Ferrari/Photoshot; 12, © Biosphoto/
Superstock; 13, © Nick Garbutt/Superstock; 14, © Vladimir Wrangel/Shutterstock, © reptiles4all/Shutterstock, and
© Edwin Verin/Shutterstock; 15, © Suzi Eszterhas/Minden Pictures/FLPA; 16, © Tim Laman/ National Geographic
Stock; 17, © Cede Prudente/Photoshot; 18, © blickwinkel/Alamy; 19, © Bruce Coleman Inc/Alamy; 20, © ANT Photo
Library/Photoshot; 21L, © Arto Hakola/Shutterstock; 21R, © Patrice Correia/Biosphoto/FLPA; 23TL, © Aleksey
Stemmer/Shutterstock; 23TC, © Tim Laman/ National Geographic Stock; 23TR, © David Yeo/Getty Images; 23BL,
© Bruce Coleman Inc/Alamy; 23BC, © reptiles4all/Shutterstock; 23BR, © Janelle Lugge/Shutterstock.

Publisher: Kenn Goin
Editorial Director: Adam Siegel
Creative Director: Spencer Brinker
Design: Emma Randall
Editor: Mark J. Sachner
Photo Researcher: Ruby Tuesday Books Ltd

*Library of Congress Cataloging-in-Publication Data*

Phillips, Dee, 1967–
  Flying lemur / by Dee Phillips.
     p. cm. — (Treed: animal life in the trees)
  Includes bibliographical references and index.
  ISBN-13: 978-1-61772-911-9 (library binding) — ISBN-10: 1-61772-911-6 (library binding)
  I. Flying lemurs—Juvenile literature.  I. Title.
  QL737.D35P45 2014
  599.33—dc23
                              2013011518

For more information, write to Bearport Publishing Company, Inc., 45 West 21st Street, Suite 3B,
New York, New York 10010. Printed in the United States of America.

10 9 8 7 6 5 4 3 2 1

# Contents

# Flying Through the Trees

In a **rain forest**, a small, furry animal clings to a tall tree trunk.

Suddenly, the creature leaps from the tree, spreading its arms and legs wide.

Large flaps of skin unfold from its body as it **glides** between trees.

The animal is a flying lemur, and it's looking for food.

flying lemur

flying lemur

flaps of skin

Flying lemurs spend their whole lives in the treetops. They sleep, look for food, and raise their babies high above the ground.

# Meet Flying Lemurs

There are two kinds of flying lemurs.

They are called the Malayan flying lemur and the Philippine flying lemur.

Both kinds live in rain forests in Asia, where it is warm all year long.

They both also have thick brown or gray fur.

Adults are about 15 inches (38 cm) long.

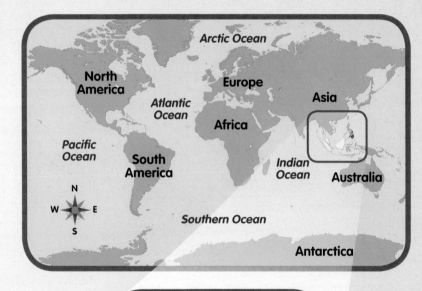

Where Malayan flying lemurs live
Where Philippine flying lemurs live

claws

Malayan
flying lemur

Flying lemurs
have curved claws
on their fingers and
toes. They use the
claws to hold on to
tree trunks and
branches.

Describe what a flying
lemur looks like to
someone who has
never seen one before.

# Built for Gliding

Flying lemurs don't really fly, like birds do.

Instead, they glide from tree to tree.

The large piece of skin that stretches between their arms and legs helps them glide.

The skin catches the air when they spread out their bodies.

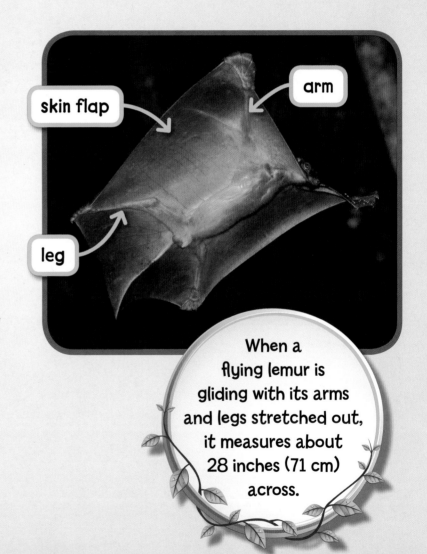

skin flap

arm

leg

When a flying lemur is gliding with its arms and legs stretched out, it measures about 28 inches (71 cm) across.

Flying lemurs have huge eyes. How do you think having large eyes helps the animal?

9

# Days and Nights

A flying lemur spends its days sleeping.

It rests clinging to a tree trunk or hanging upside-down from a branch.

As night falls, the animal wakes up to look for food.

It climbs up high in a tree, lets go, and glides to another tree.

After it finds food, it gets ready to take off by climbing up high again.

A flying lemur's large eyes help it see well in the dark. They also help the animal figure out how far away a tree trunk or branch is before it takes off.

# Time to Eat

Flying lemurs feed on the leaves, fruit, and flowers of trees.

Sometimes, they eat nectar, which is a sweet liquid made by flowers.

Flying lemurs also eat **bark**, which is the tough covering of tree trunks and branches.

Flying lemurs get water from the leaves and other foods they eat. They also lick rainwater from leaves.

How do you think flying lemurs stay safe from animals that want to eat them?

# Staying Safe

A flying lemur's fur helps it blend in with the colors of tree trunks.

If a **predator**, such as an eagle, comes close, the flying lemur stays completely still.

It looks like part of the tree trunk, so the eagle doesn't see it.

If a predator comes too close, the flying lemur glides to another tree.

**Flying Lemur Predators**

leopard

snake

eagle

Snakes, monkeys, and leopards catch and eat flying lemurs. Large birds, such as eagles and hawks, also hunt the little animals.

# Baby Flying Lemurs

Adult flying lemurs live alone until it's time to **mate**.

About 150 days after mating, a female flying lemur gives birth to a tiny baby.

The baby has no fur, and it's about the size of a mouse.

It drinks milk from its mother's body.

mother flying lemur

baby flying lemur

As a mother flying lemur glides from tree to tree, the baby travels with her. It flies through the air, clinging to the fur on its mother's belly.

baby flying lemur

A mother flying lemur has a special way of keeping her baby cozy and warm. What do you think she does?

# A Cozy Life

When resting, a mother flying lemur makes a warm, soft **pouch** for her baby.

She does this by wrapping the skin she uses for gliding around the baby.

During the first few months of life, the young flying lemur's fur grows.

By the time it's six months old, it no longer drinks its mother's milk.

Instead, it eats adult foods such as leaves and flowers.

A newborn flying lemur weighs just over one ounce (28 g). An adult flying lemur can weigh up to four pounds (1.8 kg).

mother
flying lemur

baby flying
lemur

19

# Growing Up

At six months old, a flying lemur is ready to leave its mother.

Now, it's able to glide through the air on its own.

Like all flying lemurs, it can cover a distance of 320 feet (98 m) in one leap!

It will spend the rest of its days sleeping, and its nights gliding through the rain forest.

six-month-old
flying lemur

ruffed lemur

adult flying lemur

Lemurs are furry animals that are closely related to monkeys. Flying lemurs are not actually a type of lemur. They got their name because their big eyes and pointed faces reminded people of lemurs.

21

# Science Lab

## Help Save the Rain Forest

Rain forest trees where flying lemurs live are being cut down for wood. They are also being cut down to make space to grow crops.

Without trees, flying lemurs will not be able to survive. Why? Flying lemurs cannot walk or run. They can only move by climbing trees and gliding from branch to branch.

Make a poster that tells people to stop cutting down rain forest trees. On your poster write all the reasons why flying lemurs need trees. You can draw pictures, too!

To help you think of facts to include on your poster, try answering the questions below.

• *How do flying lemurs look for food?*

• *What do flying lemurs eat?*

• *How do flying lemurs hide from predators?*

Flying lemurs need trees.
Don't cut down the rain forest!

Flying lemurs eat tree leaves, fruit, and flowers.

To find food, flying lemurs must glide from tree to tree.

# Science Words

**bark** (BARK) the tough covering of a tree's trunk and branches

**glides** (GLYEDS) to move above the ground by floating on air; gliding looks a little like flying

**mate** (MAYT) to come together in order to have young

**pouch** (POUCH) a flap of skin or pocket of skin on a mother animal's body used for carrying her young

**predator** (PRED-uh-tur) an animal that hunts and eats other animals

**rain forest** (RAYN FOR-ist) a place where many trees and other plants grow, and lots of rain falls

# Index

# Read More

**Allgor, Marie.** *Endangered Rain Forest Animals.* New York: Rosen (2013).

**Clark, Willow.** *Flying Lemurs.* New York: PowerKids Press (2012).

# Learn More Online

To learn more about flying lemurs, visit **www.bearportpublishing.com/Treed**

# About the Author

Dee Phillips lives near the ocean on the southwest coast of England. She develops and writes nonfiction and fiction books for children of all ages. Dee's biggest ambition is to one day walk the entire coast of Britain—it will take about ten months.